Emotions Into Motion

By
Jordan Blue

TABLE OF CONTENTS

Dedication v

Acknowledgments vi

Intro vii

The Letter 0

When I'm Alone 4

Yhwh 5

Spark 7

Again… 9

Nala 11

Zipporah 13

Story 16

I Write… 18

Mama 20

Black Child 22

Love Her Nature 25

Pressure God 28

Perfectionistic Curse 31

Songlasses 34

The Remote 36

Conversations With My Past 38

Truth Vs. Reality 40

How Can I? 43

New Chapters 45

Sheltered Lenses 46

Cellular Shadow 48

Hermana 50

Status Report 52

Wendy 55

I Stand 58

Why The Ocean Loves The Volcano 60

Voices 62

Dear Emotions 64

Outtro 66

DEDICATION

This book is dedicated to my beautiful wife, Analissa. You challenge me to be better every day. This is a reminder of where we used to be and how we continue to grow.

ACKNOWLEDGMENTS

I'd like to thank my family and friends who supported me in the lowest and highest times.

I also would like to thank all the dark times in my life that inspired these poems.

INTRO

These are my emotions put into a motion parallel to the Nile

Some are long, some are short, but they all come from the same aisle

I am blessed in my journey that God has provided

I know through my hardships, He is beside me

It is because of Him my demons are behind me

So that I can share my life with you with a smile

These are my emotions put into a motion as grounded as our land

Some make you smile, some make you cry, but you'll always understand

For this rhyme and reason provide a foundation

To connect with your own personal relation

Therefore, we can see all lives with more appreciation

And make an effort to give each other a chance

THE LETTER

To whom it may concern,

To the hero that inspired me since

The beginning, when God made the world lit

Remember when Mama was crying? I hate when I see that shit

Over some blatant lies, betrayal, and abandonment

You returned as a reminder of how hard this pain hit

Yet you still had the denial to think we'd forget

How you chose to leave us behind, and think you can come

back quick

Nah, that shit ain't right, and I ain't one to quickly forgive.

Who the fuck do you think you are walking in like you didn't

let us suffer

All so you can get a nut from some white girl lover

You were once a superhero on my comic book cover

But now you're just another simple ass nigga who put us under

To whom it may concern,

To the streets that struck me down to my core

The day I met you and chose to become yours

My heart pounded, and fear seeped through every pore

Anticipating my death lurking behind every door

Opening even one of them meant signing my soul forth

To a brotherhood that promised a union gutted from war

You took advantage of my loneliness and turned me into a cynic

To see everyone as my enemy, everything as a gimmick

Stripped me of my pride, to the point where I'm timid

And convince me that love is a curse that should never be given.

How dare you offer us a sense of hope when all you provide is pain,

Brainwash us to believe that we will be given respect only when we obey

You killed my friends, Jamaal and Trey, and left my ass in the streets as prey

I think about that shit every day, to where I possess demons; Piru is my rain

To whom it may concern,

I reminisce on these hardships daily slowly till I'm done breaking every piece of my heart

My innocence blinded me from reality, and a sudden glimpse of the truth tore my world apart

What baffles me is that one moment, I see a beautiful path brightened by the stars

Then the next moment, the cosmos falls upon me to leave overwhelming burns and scars

There are some days I wish I could throw up a white flag or a big ass card

That says, "HELP!! This shit is hard."

I'm confused

It's like my fears and my habits are fused

Pain caused me, and I caused pain; the cycle continues

To the extent where I can't answer the question, "what's gotten into you?"

Well, if you ask me this time, I'll know exactly what to tell you

I'm lost, I'm bothered, I'm sad, I'm hindered

I've lost all human connection, yet still connected from the lustful lurking of tinder

Seeking warm comfort in communities that give me the cold shoulder like winter

I'm sorry I stopped caring for the passions and people I love so tender.

But whatever,

I learned to live level-headed

and maintain a code imbedded in my head

to keep me steady and ready

for salvation when I'm heavied

for reconstruction eventually, so that I soon may build a fire

in my belly to tell me:

"Stay grounded so that you may rise."

"Stay grounded so that you may rise."

"Stay grounded so that you may rise."

I say that religiously with pride and with the ambition that I
can thrive
I'm grateful for its smoldering fire that shines
To persistently help me realize
That my strengths are the branches of the pain rooted inside
I am a product of my environment, but my environment is
only one factor
I am the other, and with change, I will utilize my pain to
build my plain and write a new chapter.
To whom it may concern,
Just let me say Thank You
Sincerely Jordan Ray Blue

WHEN I'M ALONE

Like a blank canvas with no paintbrushes

You try to speak but can't say nothing

Just say you straight; they don't care if you're bluffing

They say, "how are you?" but rarely stay to listen to "I'm struggling."

It's sad

You're numb from emotions, debating whether it's good or bad

You lost sight of your future, forgot the lessons of your past

Forgot all the good experiences you ever had

To find that nothing good could ever last

You're on this endless cycle of confusion, don't even remember getting on the bike

But no matter what you're blessed with, still, nothing feels right

That sparkle in your eye that was once so bright now dims to dull light.

So, you distract yourself with the sirens nectar, find comfort in her fading breath

You accept her lust and disrespect because you think what you give is what you get

Yet you give her everything until there is nothing left and

You ignore her toxic agenda till the day she introduces her true name…death.

YHWH

I believe you are real, but I cannot believe this is how you handled things.

I know someday I may understand it, but how can I when you never explain it to me.

I dream every day of your return, try to conform to your every word, and yet it seems that around every curve

The same problems tend to repeat

Every time I read your book, I don't see the love of a God.

To be honest, what I see is the duty of man and how we only have one job.

A job to care for each other, love one another, be a father, be a mother to all

But in moments when we can't even do that, where is your call

Yeah, there are stories of your powers and your miracles,

but where have you been in this generation where peace is only mythical.

Hate is universal in every language, and war takes away love and leaves anguish

Everyone is pointing fingers to where the blame is and believes their reclamation is univocal

Then call it political to hide their means to kill people, and yet undesirably, there is a sequel

A frequent pattern of murder, rape, and suicide is justified by statements like "it's a dog eat dog world" or "it's do or die."

There is no "you and I;" there's only "me and mine," yet with you in mind, we gain the courage of Nehemiah

How?

Where is courage when we build walls between our differences?

Where is patience when we obtain bliss at a moment's instance?

Where is hope of rescue when we don't even know what we're missing?

Where is love when we make a conscious effort to be so distant?

Where are you, God? When we need you the most!

Why is it that those who stray further from you feel so close?

Why are we so addicted to sin, fiending for every dose?

Why do we see each other as foes? Do you even know?

YHWH

SPARK

It begins with a spark, a light so minuscule

Hitting the ground with frailty from the friction produced

It's new, small, but created in hopes of enlightening a few

Although a sliver, the potential for its growth continues

With the breath given from our own soul, we allow it to breathe

For although broken, we can still give life in thee

We are Anomalies created to create this anomaly

This is the true evidence of God that we need.

This is meant to break any man-made policy

Now you see....

After its creation, we are not finished.

The moment we believe we are, our masterpiece is diminished.

Yes, God rested on the seventh day, but He still hasn't accepted His commission

For He knows, and we too shall know, that we are never through with this mission.

It must become a passion so consistent, so listen

Your efforts in this exposition must be so persistent

For there will be days where its flame will glisten

But other moments seem to keep you feeling distant.

The quality of effort you put into its raise is vital.

For if you force it with toxins, it will run wild

The initial cost to its flame may seem so mild

Until you see the pain it causes within its subtitle

For this creation between two creations hurts, the struggle is inevitable

But with the right mindful efforts, the struggle can be credible

Trust the process; longevity requires work that's gradual

And understand this flame is a part of God's schedule.

Soon enough, you will see the benefits of your sweat and tears

And begin to appreciate the blood sacrificed to bring you here

From the warmth and light, you are now enjoying from near

You can realize that there is simply nothing to fear.

So…spark.

AGAIN...

All four of her limbs wrap around me, like coils surrounding
my body

With three simple words, she has managed to kill me softly

My two hands hold her naked thighs as I look straight into
her eyes and lay

One threshold is opened by the key of our foreplay.

Our caressing bodies relay friction that creates a spark, a
type of fiction that's unreal

The profound melody of her moans as I flow deep within her
bones like sweet chamomile

Our balanced natures meet with passions so complete that
nothing competes with our yin and yang

My wildfire makes her oceans and lakes stand still and quake
as we begin to take the time away

Time is nonexistent when I lie with her, and so is the world
around us

Just two souls being exchanged between locked covenants
of a kiss to allow trust.

Yet, at the cusp of this lustful journey through her voluptuous
land

I reach the climax of her story as she slowly cringes in my
hands

This is not the end, but the beginning of a new plan, so understand

That this event will happen again...and again...and again.

NALA

I can sense the joy through your imaginary eyes, and I cry

Blissful tears flow parallel to my love as I realize you are mine

Although never acquainted, I've known you my entire life

You've been in my dreams ever since my thoughts could be televised

I'm in love—fallen into the quicksands of time

Descending rapidly as I watch you grow

Moments I wish I could softly shift the paradigm

So I can get one last glimpse of your glow

But just know that you will reap what I sew

You shall inherit the very essence that stems within my bones

My beloved daughter, you shall inherit this enlightened throne

Embrace this legacy and learn to carry on

God has gifted me with you and your mother, a blessing indeed

There is truly no greater love but hers and mine for our benevolent seed

You proceed to seize every heartbeat within me with the sound of your laugh

I promise to be honest and constant as I possibly can be to smoothen your path

Perhaps, I can even get a chance to glance at you walking steadily for the first time

Or perhaps, I even get a chance to dance with you at your wedding; where is the time

You shine brighter than any light higher than I can envision

I reminisce on my regrets with a readiness to say, "Good Riddance."

I am overzealous to be over hellish behavior as a role model in your mission

For I know God only creates beauty, and you prove to be His evidence

ZIPPORAH

I have to say this

I have an admiration for the patience she gave to this nation

Courageously facing the hateful faces raging against her creation

They're irately racing to erase her race for her greatness intimidates them

But she's amazing, irreplaceable

A beast with beauty untamable

Her wild thoughts blow shots at the thoughts that believe she's ever incapable

Melanin overcasts her temple, but her light excels on all levels, overwhelming the shadows

She's an example, but for her grace, we are ungrateful

Get tasteful of her faithful love and be shameful of your wasteful lust

For temporary crumbs, rather than indulge in her cherry and plums

And trust that her radiant sun can be loving but painful

A Godsend Queen, Lioness of the jungle with cubs to feed

She plans to succeed with the intention to provide what we need.

God oversees His daughters of Eve and is pleased with His angels.

Black women, I appreciate you, there is no denying that

But I decline to listen to their false lines of how they hate your ass

Because they don't, they hate that they're not you, in fact

They throw slight jabs to hide their desire to be you so bad

While in the back, they braid their hair and give each other slight tans

It's sad, but I laugh

For boys underestimate your impact on this world

Replacing aspirations for your wisdom and power with their thirst for your curves

Their ignorant desperation for your flesh is exposed by their superficial actions and words

We as men need to learn that

In the view of a brother, nothing is better

Than the plethora of pleasure

She gives to a fella when he lets her

And she will let him know that she will never let him go

Such as the love Martin got from Coretta

So please, don't please us

Teach us

How to treat you like the Queen you are

Believe in us

In that, we may mend your scars

Forgive us

For causing those from afar

And last but not least, raise us

To be the Kings you know we are

STORY

A story scatters in different directions as if spewed from the seed of a Balsam Fir

Spreading ferociously to attach itself to a host willing to listen

Diverse perspectives intercept the roots and branch it out with their own personal word

But rarely choose to seek the benefits of reconnecting

Don't we see that it is a blessing to learn a lesson from our peers?

We are all here together with the same fears of being alone

It does not make us any less than any of the next men or women if we open an ear

Understanding others' lives provides authentic life rather than building fake minds of silicone

Without the wholesome nature of acceptance held prone to the stairway to the heavens we know

From tales of testimonies, lines of holy matrimonies, I pray that you may know me and what I love and

I shall reciprocate my heart, or even initiate this to start, so that we may mend our scars with true blood

We are above all this! Do you not see?

My tears match yours, and your smiles match mine; we share identities

Yes, we are individual in our intersectionality, but please believe

That there is a bigger picture of this world's puzzle, and we are just a piece!

Can we be at peace?!

We are brothers and sisters, for love's sake

But love is at stake if we continue to drive a stake in each other's core

I do not pray for more; I do not pray for a house on the shores; I pray that we can go forth and multiply

And I don't just mean from friction between two bodies but indeed between two open minds

Is it a crime to believe that two souls can intertwine in a tapestry so beautiful?

For one time, can we look through God's eyes rather than rely on the limited sight from our cubicles?

It is too simple, but we choose to make it so complicated

We are outdated from our shameless fears of changes that we try to tame it, but resistance is futile.

Just embrace the fact that you are an important chapter in HIS story, and that is what makes you useful.

I WRITE...

I write

To reflect God's light through my river of words

I write

To escape this abyssal estate that wanders

My mind

Overwhelmed by the waves flipping me backward

I might

Go insane if I don't exhale these statements, so...

I write

My wrongs within my soul are poured out from the seams

Gashing as if my confessions have sliced straight through
my veins

Flowing from my wrist down to the tip of the quill, I bleed

In hopes that my efforts do not seize in vain,

I claim

I ponder, and I cogitate on everything

Belabored by my conscience to further add more things

To paint an HD portrait of what I perceive

So that one day you may soon understand me

Because this is me, this is my pain

This is my happiness, this is my shame

This is all my emotions compiled in a matter of days

So that years later, you may remember my name

I do not write to escape oblivion; I write to embrace the truth

We are all beautiful, and nothing remains new

But words can travel farther than the eye can see

I choose to write my future dynasties

And with deliverance, yet said so silently

I say quietly, I believe in you

I write

So that you may read

I write

So that you may see

That we all have a basic need

To release the inner words we keep.

I Write…

MAMA

Necessary, I find it, to give credit to her smile

Most definitely the holiest picture I will see in a lifetime

For through countless adverse moments, where screams, cries, and groans tend

To gather and zone in, that smile has remained focused

She has taught me what true strength is about

My mother is the first Queen I have seen, identified and confirmed

When I learned how confidently she discerned

Her reliance on the Most High instead of confiding in the limited heights

That men can't climb and resign her life to Him, and not to him

She is true kin to true love, for her care is pure, that of the Lamb

There is nothing more I could ever ask for than the basking embrace of her hands

I know some may understand when I say that I forget a lot of shit (excuse my language)

But Forreal, I forget to turn in homework, slack in doing my own chores, and lose track of when

my next game is

But I will never forget her faces, especially the ones of laughter and amazement

I will never forget her gracious voice toned and sewed into every statement

I don't remember much when I was a baby

But I can tell you exactly how she held me then because that is how she holds me now

And how she will continue to hold me as time counts down

Ain't that wild? How all this was born from her smile?

And I don't mean this poem, I mean the story

Of two humans joining in communion, forming a covenant for union

To fix a fusion of genetic data in the movement to prove His power

This all started with her smile! So, I find it necessary to give credit to it.

Without that smile, this child could never be here

So, let me be clear when I say that smile will always be dear to my heart,

I love you, Mama, and you will always be the greatest of God's art.

BLACK CHILD

Birth occurs twice, my black child

The first is in the eyes of the world; now able to classify you and define you with a few words

Based on your surface, they place you on a stage like a merchant and predestine your purpose

With preconceived notions of what your worth is

If you white, you're worth this

If you not, you're worthless

Undeserving of reimbursement for the curses coerced unto you with perverseness

And whether you like it or not, you surrender, for that's how it works here

That's how society moves no matter who you were created to be

They speculate your origin to regulate your portion of this nation's feed

They feed you lies and fallacies of who they intend you to be

When the truth is they have no control in the least yet

We're prisoners to the chains of predestined stereotypes, yet we choose to guard them

Stanford's experiment is not just limited to prisoners and guards, you see?

"Your ancestors' slavery has been abolished" is just a polished way of cropping our pain

Out of their history, to hide the mystery of our stolen hearts like gashes hidden by a band-aid

They think we stupid like we were born yesterday

When our minds have aged with more than books from a class

Kunta Kinte said "Toby" just to get that whip off his back, not because that whip made his mind break

For Birth occurs twice, my black child

The second birth is of your own making; a moment of revelation,

Rejuvenated from the second wind after you hit rock bottom from your relation to sin

This momentous occasion is the replacement of your complacence with societal expectations with a desire to change it.

Rebirth is the realization that your true worth is not where they placed you but where you place yourself

You create your legacy; you write your story; you define your wealth

You do this on your own; you don't need their help

A butterfly doesn't break its cocoon with the help of the branch that holds it

Break the chains that leash you in!

Shed the skin they leave you in!

Escape the cage they see you in and observe their fear as they see you win!

And when you done, tell them, "here, hold this!"

Be focused and hone in on your spiritual potency,

For these stanzas are not just for you to admire my lyrical fluency

Let those in power be the ones that read my words foolishly

While you self-reflect on your inherent royalty instead of their disparaging

Perceptions of you seeming meek as slaves when you were Kings and Queens that gave

The wisdom and knowledge that paid

For their ignorance that could have sent them to their graves

Let this day be your birthday, black child.

LOVE HER NATURE

The Sum of her parts was ever-changing as the parting from Summer

To Fall for her meant my life rearranged from present sun to clouded smother

My calling for sure sent passions to her in a fashion of Winters wind manifesting cold days

As she answers my cry, I Spring for her reborn embrace, and I realized

As seasons change, so shall I

Genocide of thoughts that before pushed love aside from calm shores

Where Malice undercurrents attempt raging tides to drown any sense of life

But what was once a small pebble of infatuation with accreditation from the Lord

Now leaves adoration at the midst of bountiful coasts…I am hers…and she is mine

She values the matters of the mind and derives every emotion from her Creator

This is why I love Him because He took His eternal time to make her.

And saved her…just for me, because He knew me.

He knew that I would notice every detail of pleasurable moments in His poetic masterpiece

He predestined my gentle hands would caress her precious land with copacetic peace

And through exploration within her spiritual nation, I discover the most romantic thing

At the same time, I am surrounded with honey; she as well is in love with me.

Naturally comes friction between us; igniting addiction for crushed hearts

Sacrificial lives are only willing when a true covenant in fire is sparked

For accepting the pain in hopes of heavenly exchange is why I take bark

From her strong roots to her fig leaves, I plan to love all her parts.

Lord Most High

Mother Nature

Father Time

I love her nature

I find favor in her innocence, and I cater to her significance

Not with complacency but with content patience, she will reciprocate my labor

She is my equal in every field but provides different fruits to balance my yield

I obtain the true substance from her every meal so that I am strong enough to be her shield.

Feeling her tender presence, no matter the chasms between every distance

Allows me to fathom her pleasant senses and trust that her passion holds persistence

She is the result of a perfect instance, where my self-growth intersected with God's mission

Though the Sum of her parts are ever-changing as the parting from Summer

Lord knows I wake up every morning with a constant aching to say, "I love her."

As the seasons changed...

PRESSURE GOD

Ever recall a moment of pure bliss?

Sense of true adoration for life in the pursuit of happiness?

Momentous magnificence in the perception of self-reflection,

Blessed by the lessons learned to make you better than you were

More enduring to pain, evident by assuring faith displayed through your words

Yet your actions speak exorbitantly louder with every footstep

Jubilation tied at the bootstraps of an exuberant mind whom at Arduous times, your elation remains heard?

Yeah…me neither.

I know how it is

They say ignorance is bliss

This is probably why the knowledge we possess stimulates discomfort

Especially when the information we acquire only inspires us to inquire about others' credibility to confirm

Sparking doubt from the friction between facts and truth, we lose track of who's the priest and who's the fool

Or if the priest is the fool, and glass disguises itself as a jewel

We ask, "Where is our fuel if we are the tools that build God's mass?

Where is the rouge from the sacrificed King that God uses to paint our flesh?

Where is our sense of gratitude when we don't feel like the rescued, just the wreck?"

We wrestle with our heresy until it chokes us to death

But let me tell you this:

If you are in the middle of your interrogation with God

And you fear that once He is cornered by your exposition of His flaws

He will strike you with a lightning bolt and declare, "that's enough of your bull-"

Nah! I implore you to keep asking

The power of your agnostic pressure only forms the diamond we call devotion

That is the boat rocking steadily within the wrath of thunderous oceans

The meek standing strong amid massive forces

That is a galaxy created from bright stars torn open

That is GOD, walking alongside you possessed with love ready to adorn thee.

You get me?

Understand that faith and love are parallel universes with the same odyssey

Both a passion for braving through demons with a balance
of confidence and modesty

Withholding the vows of loyalty, support, and honesty

Promising to persist a covenant beyond eternal days,

Bestow faith in your love and love in your faith.

This is the Way,

The Truth,

The Life,

Do not fret in your suspicion, for it is this way that your truth
shall come to life.

Even Jesus asked why

When His Father had forsaken Him at the end of His time

Though He knew the Gates of Heaven were but a threshold
established by sacrifice.

PERFECTIONISTIC CURSE

Perfection! A nonexistent standard that is only defined by perception.

Absolute solely on the assumed character of our Creator in the heavens.

Impossible to achieve as a human due to our consistent inconsistencies.

Well, in that case, why do I always stress to be…perfect?

Combining expectations both external and inside me

Driving enough voices crying to diagnose anxiety

And keep me thriving in the environment of a mental asylum

My body is a furnace that constantly pressures my heart and mind in

Searing thermal forces, my coal mines pan full of diamonds

Correction, my cold mind painfully dies, man!

I've gone miles in a second to provide a single answer to a question

Second-guessing my profession so that my actions hold the power of a historic message

Persistently testing my wisdom as a youth when I still have lessons to learn

This eternal blessing of free will, the gift to discern, is ironically my curse

My lips locked in pursed position as I am cyclically told that
I am human
With well-understood misconceptions that is typically the
mold we've concluded
And accepted with exception to our spiritual predisposed
solution
Still, I self-projected my requirements critically to hold that
of omnipotence
I am not the second coming! So why do I compare myself
to it?
I'm clueless, but I hide within intellectual illusions and
I'm new to every experience, yet handle it as if I've been
through this shit
I'm spooked by failure that I fight for my life to achieve
fruition.
My breath evades me at the very thought of losing it.
But I'm losing myself in the avoidance of bruising myself.
My mental health is overwhelmed by the helm of pursuing
wealth.
I tend to be the only one who breaks every sculpture I build
Solely so I can have enough fragments to forge a shell
I am not well, yet I am at the apex of my species
Completing every task efficiently but lack the proficiencies
to complete me

I am never satisfied with my achievements; instead, I identify with this indifferent disease

That leaves me bleeding for a cause self-proclaimed with grievance motivating greed.

Help me! No! I don't need help; your assistance is unnecessary.

I find my panic and stress as a tentative mist that is only temporary.

I discard my discretions with ambitions to keep my weapon ready

So disregard my decay and ignore my screams for sanctuary I'll be fine

I declare as my stare is bare naked with tears from the tears of my skin as I shear every flaw from my flesh

Till the only thing that's left is the memory of an empty canvas

SONGLASSES

The prayers of legends transcend that of the masses

Therefore, passion was only formed in a profound fashion

The sands of time are pressured by searing flames, washed

by clearing rains, excess departed by winds astray

To leave diamond lenses hooked to a brass string

An accessory so necessary, used to expose temporary desires

And enlighten those who choose to wear them

Allowing the ordinary to see much higher

David could see he needed faith so that he may fight his giants

Solomon could discover his wish for the wisdom of Xion

Buddha could live a life that would later open his eyes and

Soon I may truly understand who I am

The transparency of knowing our needs is less apparent

when we lose focus in Thee

We are left blinded by surfaced dividers

The pursuit of happiness, love, and strength

Is covered by the zeal for satisfaction, lust, and fame

Our own aspirations deliberately lie to us

But Truth overcomes only when we take a second glance

If we were to brush the surface; see past the tempting

incursions

Put First Things First, then our second things will not be

suppressed but enhanced

So give it a chance, put on these "Songlasses"

And I don't mean for the Sun that brightens our days; I mean for the Son that brightens our ways

In that, we may not be led astray but instead act as if we were molded by His clay

So the next time you pray…

Do not pray for a new car; pray for faith and that you may travel far.

Do not pray for currency; pray for hope and that you may spread it superfluously

Do not pray for success; pray for love and that you may reveal how truly you are blessed.

THE REMOTE

Can someone please explain to me why this remote never works for me? Does it work for you?

No matter what button I press, nothing seems to happen the way I urge it to

Listen, I try to increase the volume of my actions, but I still lose sound

I attempt to channel my emotions, yet I still feel down

I try to get input in my life, but I don't know how

I'm seriously about to launch this worthless tool

And maybe I should...

Maybe I should toss this remote, pass it to a host who truly has the control

And maybe He can do me good.

Maybe I need to understand that it is not the remote, but it is my hands that can't possess the Power that He could

Wait! Am I insisting that I give up my life to decrease the wares of my worth?!

Kneel to the care of His Myrrh; yield and bare society's curse?

Be weak among affairs of extrinsic thirst?

Wasn't it Jesus who said the meek inherits the Earth?

What if being invincible means I understand the principle of being indivisible from God

What if instead of selling my soul to human nature, which provides instant satisfaction.

I surrender my control to the Creator, who promises greater than that bliss

Just a thought

God alone can speak volumes into my soul

Channel enough energy to make me whole

Input the love I put in plus ten-fold

At the cost of simply giving Him the remote.

CONVERSATIONS WITH MY PAST

I don't know you, nor does your acquaintance meet mine

Strangers parted by the intersection of space and time

And yet everything you do brings me to this exact moment

Blessed to hold potency to owning my choices

Although unfortunate to never catch my glance

You still hold my attention with the extension of your emotion

Your passions reside within my mind

I don't know you, and your eyes lack the sight of my own

The memory of you tends to fade slow

But the connection between us never seems to whither

The paralleled souls in sync rarely hindered

The touch of your wisdom falling into my hands

I shall soar in clouds of wonder and glorious bounds from

under the wings shaped by your feather.

I shall reap what you sow

I don't know you, nor have you recalled me

Our stories prove forgotten eventually

Still, together we follow through with a mission

To give everything we have, everything we are in submission

To pass the ones who come after us the gift of chance

I realize what you hope for me is the power in victory, like
that I wish in them
My love was yours originally
Conversations with my past.

TRUTH VS. REALITY

Lies! Lies! Lies!

The enemy mascots that break my relationship

But I shall mirror the wrath of Armageddon's cry

And spread Biblical truth, knocking the demons into the eternal abyss

For I am amidst the bliss of heaven's innocence

Able to defeat my foes with ease as my perception understands what is right

It's not that difficult to fight with confidence

When common sense helps bring sin into the light

But why is it I still see pain, fear, injustice distributed in the world today

Leaving the poor to pay, voices with no say

Love is used in vain to abuse Eve's temple for Adam's gain

A King's reign is shortened by poisoned rains and toxic steams

All because lies are less apparent when interwoven into reality

Death in Battle is justified by a good cause

For we know the lives of humans will balance the weight of fuel's cost

A woman is stripped of her dignity by cultural laws

For she is a marketable object meant to sell; prohibit her flaws

The skin of an individual is a warning sign to provoke prejudice

Or shall I say caution... Do you see what's wrong here?

Deceptions have been fabricated into convictions,

To the extent where religion is seen as an antagonist to success

And happiness is a selfish pursuit to be above everything but my own sentiment

But that's okay! That's just the way it is. Accept it!

We take advantage of dependence to come before faith

We claim subject to God's predicate

I don't think y'all hear me,

Let me slow it down for you

Nothing that is... is the way it should be... if it doesn't support the truth

This is nothing new, yet its hidden proof, slipped under and through

Crevasses at the bottom of dead pools filled with liquid foolishness

Yet despite the horrid depths, Elohim reached for its breath, stood before you with this text,

And still, we ask, "what do we do with it?" Even as we witness the descent of maroon

Realize that the power of Real Lies will not be victorious for Real Eyes

The Eyes of disciples in truth

Now, can anyone tell me the Keyword of this message?

Truth that's the lesson!

Yet this world is built on a foundation of reality without knowing its harm

When Reality actually stands for

Residents who Easily Assimilate to the Lust for Inner Temptation's Yarn

A life in Reality is a lie, but a life in the Truth is alive.

HOW CAN I?

How can I say that I am saved?

When I still choose to remain sin's slave

No one earthly event can raise me up from my personal commission

My heart stays heavy from the anchor of shame

Guilt and angst drown me in sorrowful rains

And train me to be holy in vain

And claim to be satisfying to the brain

When chains hold my soul to tantalizing dreams

It's me, who is the enemy of me.

Some call it ego, but He goes to reveal its true name- Evil

I need full honesty when rebuking my Kingdom

He knows that we constantly try to reach for freedom

But it's pointless when I do it alone,

For how can I escape another world without knowing my home?

I'm prone to worldly ambitions and motion for sensual submission

Lose intimacy within wholesome relations till all my compassion is gone

Depressing to think about

But when did grace ever start tasting like the sweetness of a honeycomb

Whoa! Revelations of an individual, when God's name remains residual

Love unconditional surpassing human acceptance

Not changed for the better, I took for granted God passing over me

My body remains unleavened

I was given mercy when I deserved the wrath of the heavens

My palms remain clean at the cost of His hands severed

I ask for forgiveness when it has already been given

What I was missing was my part in truly repenting

God, please level me, put me in my place

With the balance of seeing both love and hate on my face

Deliver me from this sensational cage,

For if I still look for my gain, how can I say that I am saved?

NEW CHAPTERS

New chapters condone chaos of components

The moonlight gleaming an outline of divine intervention

With high tides from our struggle to abide by guidelines

And a timeline that remains limited

Commotions between waves and trenches are moments in our oceanic glories.

No author presents an exposition with happily ever after

Because "after" never really happens

It just so happens the presence of happiness is the absence of a true story

SHELTERED LENSES

The eye is never naked,

For constantly, its sight is slightly shaded

Filtered and faded by close-minded behavior

Jittered and jaded with resistance to failure

Especially blind to see that changes occur inevitably

Eventually, blind to see that difference doesn't make you my enemy

Narcissism forms hierarchical systems to soon construct societal prisms

To imprison our fates with addictions for purpose within the confines of "-isms"

So that my body defines the foundations of my character

My skin positions my rightful place in America

My age determines whether I should think I'm small

My environment destines whether I should think at all

I'm appalled

This wasn't supposed to be us at all

We were created to revolutionize the making of a united nation

Where Diversity met University to build not a tower of religion but a bridge of relation

I'm frustrated that our programs of education enforce the means of separation

Knowledge and wisdom were meant to reveal that together

we rise, yet apart we fall

Still, our vision is clothed with the desire to be individual

Not for the sake to be among, but to be above

Although every rose is lathered with distinctive petals,

They are all given with the purpose of love.

So, expose your eyes to the light in which we all fall under

As one, we shall win, turn to your spring for summer

Widen your peripherals to observe countless wonders

Just imagine what we could see with our eyes uncovered.

CELLULAR SHADOW

Distractions of an idol possessed with idle hands

Cracked screens display vital concessions to grant societal demands

We praise the sidebar embedded on a case rather than the bright stars invented within our space

We have lost true appreciation for the high-cost creation of our beautiful lands

For we refuse to face the complex structure of contours, fractures, and indents

Present in body, but our minds have managed to evade incidence

For to reflect means I must expose the flaws referred to by man-made precedence

So instead, I'll settle with the dismemberment of my soul that was heaven sent

For the exchange of access to recycled standards of the internet

We are caught in a system's web

Paralyzed by tantalizing pictures overwhelming with surprising mixtures

Of moments that stimulate our perceptions without compassion, we become reckless

And lose track of our blessings, lured by the predator's breath

Put your phone down for a second!

Notice the cold hands holding it, realize its potent forces

Find you can do something more with the vascular motors in your veins as it courses

This is your day to open new doors and close old apps

Take advantage of your free will; stop waiting for Siri to react

In fact, don't seek technological permission; just listen

To the consistent beats per minute as you envision a future of ambition

Which was hidden by industrial submission

This is your moment to shine! Let your light glow!

Don't get caught behind the cellular shadow.

HERMANA

I pray she notices her impact

The greatness of her love that we all tend to lack ourselves

She sees the benefit in all without a disingenuous veil

She inhales persecution from the world without reason to tell

Yet exhales peace that spreads like a nostalgic smell

She is the fragrance that compels me

Broken by my endeavors, she is the trust that rebuilds me

In the face of danger, I hold no fear of what hell brings

For it is her loving grace that stands to help me

I'm filthy, yet in her eyes, I am clean

Like stainless steel, her pure perspective heals me

And like stainless steel, I vow to protect her at all costs

My conviction as her sole defender shall never rot

She is the epitome of resembling the blessing of God

From her source begot, my strength is wealthy

From me alone, she receives love that surpasses words

But it expands with the love she gets from the rest of the world

For she is more than a girl with talent

She is born in the spirit like a pearl amid the Atlantic

Mind, body, and soul, she represents the gift of balance

From the chasms of this blindness comes the light of her birth.

She is the daughter of a Queen who fought through many adversities

She is the daughter of a King who sought for the power in redemption

She is the friend of many who provides grace without scarcity

She is my sister, and her life to me is truly a blessing

STATUS REPORT

Status Report!

A statement of madness reformed in a systematic resort

We call business while missing the vision of what the true mission of the business is

Which is to connect of some sort.

Instead, we find comfort in sorting endless files rather than pouring endless smiles

Relationships are limited to the confines of a cellular database, while our

Real faces split far from the inner confines of our cellular human race

We paralleled a universe where our one fear of robots taking over has come true.

I mean, just look at this place.

I pace back and forth in my safe space and catch myself pondering what it's like to escape

This chrome bubble of radiation and choose to embrace

A light that doesn't just shine on my face but a light that shines today

Oh, and how scary that shit is!

Can you imagine something pure exposing your every flaw and imperfection in daylight?

What cruel and unusual punishment against my right!

That's why I like this device because it only shows my flaws
to me, and I can decide who else can see

Plus, it only reveals my surfaced appearance and not my
heart because I'm dead inside.

Oh, is that T.M.I.? Luckily I got a 4G phone that can withstand
every bit of information

And supply a rhythm of distraction for my mind with no
hesitation

So that instead of worrying about injustice residing in this
nation

I can look at new trends and plan my next vacation

Okay then,

I'll just turn my head away from people and stare at a screen
advertising the next sequel

Comparing the powers between two heroes and posting
about how this world is evil.

Because it's easier to post than it is to post up

It's easier to declare your stance than it is to stand tough

It's easier to bark through a glass fence than it is to confront

God, when did real life begin to be too rough?

It's easier to text "I love you" than it is to confess it in person

It's easier to like posts of suffering children than it is to
serve them

It's easier to show how perfect you are on the surface,

When the truth is everything within you is what is worth it.

Everything this object provides, you deserve more

You deserve a purpose and a reason you're here for

The moment unity shows its true name to this world

Is the moment we build a righteous rapport rather than a status report

WENDY

I once talked about stories, so I'll share one of mine

I was in a nice Chrysler 300 consisting of me, my pops, and my sister

Persistently pressuring my pops that on the way to Grand mama's house

We can take a detour to the wondrous place of McDonald's

With his decision, I was unable to realize then that my innocence would be shifted.

You see, all my life, I've witnessed my family accomplish remarkable wonders

In a world that intentionally forced our black pride down.

And yet, through all the success, they've achieved through adversity

They chose to turn around and give back by serving communities.

At a young age, I thought that was awesome. I got to build friendships with people less fortunate than I

Never truly realizing what it felt to be less fortunate than I

Because I complain a lot about how I'm not where I want to be or

I don't possess the attributes I want to have

I still worry, to this day, about what I don't see in front of me

Until I look back on the blessings from my past.

But back to my story,

So my pops finally decides to set our course to this palace of cheap and unhealthy substance

And you should've seen the excitement on our childish faces as we fumble in.

We get in line, wait patiently, then order: "Can I get the 10 McNuggets?" I thought I was a big boy then

Then we wait patiently for this God-given fast food to be presented

And then there it was... 10 Golden nuggets formed too perfect to be real chicken, but I didn't care

I just had a pure joy for these small masterpieces; you could see it in my stare

As I lifted one toward my mouth, my perception shifted, though

For just a few feet away, I saw a woman whose pain and age became her foe

From the looks of the tears strolling down her face and the sound of defeat descending to her base,

You felt that she had no home, let alone an identity, an identity to call her own

What prevented me from minding my business and taking a bite of my own pleasure

Was my fixation on the fact that this woman didn't have the strength to lift a feather

And yet she was trying to lift herself up from those raggedy red, white, and yellow benches

I realized that behind my blessing was someone's heart severed

I walked up to that lady, and with my pre-teen strength, I picked up her cane

I lifted her up, asked if she was okay

Then I had the courage to ask her name; I still remember it to this day

Her name was "Wendy."

I remember how ironic it was, for at the time we chose to go to McDonald's, I met a "Wendy."

After I gave her my food because I couldn't stand the thought that she could barely stand at all

Then we went our separate ways; I got in the front seat with my pops and my sister in the back

And we drove away from Wendy as she ate my Chicken Nuggets with Ranch

It started to rain as we drove away, and I knew exactly why,

Because God was crying as He saw His daughter cry

I don't know Wendy's life or what she did, or even if she is still alive

I just know that I love her, and I thank her

For I gave her strength to last the day, she gave me the purpose to last a lifetime.

I STAND

I once heard that if you stand for nothing, you'll fall for anything

They never mentioned the gravity of society that would pressure me

To sit back down and stay in my lane of entertaining

Everybody else with my talents and athletic ability

Like I'm some kind of gladiator amidst a colosseum

Volunteering my body for mindful strategy and

Spectator approval like, "do I wanna see him?"

Or "is she even good?" or "can we even beat them?"

Then came the kneeling, a moment of conflict and reason

You saw it as a potential for treason

I saw it as a chance to be me then

For I am more than an athlete

I am more than a student in a classroom

I am more than the sponsors on my feet or the mascot that represents my school

I am a strong black boy, an ambitious Latina girl,

A passionate Asian child, a motivated white child; I am the future of this world.

So I shall not back down

I shall have my voice

I stand... when I kneel

I stand… when the truth is revealed

I stand… for the freedom of our people

I stand… for the Kingdom of His people

I stand… to embrace equality

I stand… to be an anomaly

I stand… so that I can be amongst the few

I stand… so that others can stand too

WHY THE OCEAN LOVES THE VOLCANO

I love you, my volcano, and there is no doubt about that.

Even when your arms stretch and scorch my tides

Emitting steam that you see as entertainment when really it's

a painful payment

I am willing to make it in order to be in your presence.

I mean, just the essence of your heat warms my shores

To an extent where I fiend patient for more, but as you get

closer, your core

Burns me slow, leaving marks on me that you don't know

Only because I don't want to tell you.

You hear enough how your behavior is that of a hot-headed,

cantankerous

Piece of work, and it's dangerous to try to tame the flames

of your earth

And I know if I wanted to, I could wave your hellish blaze

with a tsunami of curses

But it's not worth it. Because in my teary eyes, you are perfect.

You were created in a form that bursts with an extensive

warmth and light

So torrid that when it meets my raw touch, we create lands

that can inhibit a beautiful sight.

Despite the pain, the feelings you give just feel so right.

And the way you give life to those that can't stay in my depth for long

It opens my eyes to a balance stronger than yin and yang

I belong to you, you to me

So, please don't question how one like you could be loved by one like me

Because our love was bound to happen naturally

Do not fear my pain; I am big enough to handle it, for my character

Is vast beyond measure

Forgive me when my waves become too much; I only do what I am created to do

As you are, give me time to be true, and I shall return to my gentle mute

And with the flow of my estuary, I promise to smoothen your grounded sanctuary

VOICES

I find solace in the siren

Her voice is of a lustful lyre singing melody in a minor

She lures my body to levitation as I float toward her
seductive scent

Despite my understanding that her intent carries no benevolence

Her beauty is a toxin, slowly caressing down the hairs of my skin

She takes advantage of my loneliness

My desperation is fuel to her fire

I find dependence on the Demon

His firm tone remains adamant as the behemoth

He dominates my senses to the extent where all I know

Is the rhythm of his chords that drown out my ode

To joy and peace so that I ultimately lose self-control

He leads me to where my soul I loathe

I burn till I lose all sense of healing

You tell me I'm not worthy

You tell me the foundation I built my life on is unsturdy

You hurt me with wording to expose the fears that keep me
up until 2:30

You're lurking within the murky depths of my pain

Flirting with the idea of me going insane

Any stain, red or black, reflects the darkest day of which I had

Combatting the anticipation of righting my wrongs

I thought it was only right that I write them in this poem

All I hear are the voices

All they say is that I am weak, alone, and hated

All these God-damned noises

All visualized in a clear kaleidoscope dream to leave me faded

See the demons they toy with me

Use me for their own personal utility till I'm jaded

So don't be koi with me

I don't want your pity or consolation

I want the truth, and at the same time, I have it

I'm tired of hiding; I'm done with all that masked shit

My mind is in a swampish valley

I'm not the man I thought I was, but I hope I still can be

Because me, myself, and I are not so much a lullaby as before

For it is I that nullifies the means of my growth so

That myself can remain the me I used to know.

Solace and Dependence shall soon be within my own soul

DEAR EMOTIONS

I want to tell you the truth, but who are we fooling

It's not a surprise that we both already knew it

Despite our need for each other, I see your leeched smother, and I know

That you are the part of me I don't want anything to do with

But I have no choice; you stay and manipulate my voice

And I push you away but continue to pursue me for days on end

No matter what shade I'm in, you aspire to fade right in

Quite frankly, I'm done with the bullshit

You flourish in the abyss of my thoughts

And curtain your darkness with the face of a consultant

And to admit I'm lost is certain to magnify your maladaptive potent

You're hoping I fail that I can see it in your stare, and yet you still convince me otherwise

For coping with these stale, painful memories is hell, so I choose to remain ill-advised

I compromise with your evil disguised with a veil, knowing I won't get my end of any bargain

You're just carnage, and accepting I am your victim is the hardest habit to break

For I have it engraved in my head with times I have mistakes that have left

Emotional lakes filled with blood stemmed from those I
chose to hate instead of love

It's shameful, but I choose to wade the froth

And let the waves throw me to the rocks

Despite my wish to get rid of you

It's times like these where I feel like you're all I've got.

OUTTRO

These are my emotions put into a motion as firm as a mountain

My journey in faith sends words surrounding

As delpiberation and malintent confide

I move in the story of my Savior Christ

Reborn in the biblical definition of being alive

My Rock glistens from the waters of the Holy fountain

These are my emotions put into a motion as genuine as Creation

For God was a poet: His Word the communion of nations

My path is established by perpetual growth

I seek to fulfill this eternal soul

Break bread with disciples and transcendental host

These words are meant to have my soul meet your acquaintance

Made in the USA
Las Vegas, NV
01 July 2022